Stories To Tell

Arshat M

BookLeaf Publishing
India | USA | UK

Presentation by *BookLeaf Publishing*

Web: www.bookleafpub.com

E-mail: info@bookleafpub.com

ISBN: 9789363318861

First edition 2025

To my old man—whose story I have yet to tell.

STORIES TO TELL

Of Words

You're no stranger to the old worlds—
stories of kings and kingdoms,
of Homer, and perhaps even Enheduanna.

Enheduanna, she, the first of authors,
penned more than most.

Pause.
It is no story to fit in a few lines.
Then again, no story fits in just a few lines.

This is of the word itself.
Let me be kind—think not of the first word.
Trace not back to creation,
trace not back to evolution.

Think not of the Habilis nor the Erectus.
Think not that long.

Think of Homer,
and of Enheduanna,
and of their old ones
who made up words.

Probable—all words were mere grunts at first.
But what of the first ones they made up?

If the first word could speak,
could it utter any coherence?
Like the genie escaping the lamp—
because you wish with words—
what stories would it tell?

Of the Lake

There's a big deep lake with stories to tell.
No one's ever heard one or told us how they fell.

On a moonlit night, it's just wind hushing.
Have you ever felt that eerie sense of company?

The lake speaks to you—
calling out, yet trying to push you away.
But you draw in, calming somehow,
your lungs swell as you breathe that wet air.

You don't reckon that you love that fear.
Into that lonely love, you want to dive deep,
yet you just stand and stare,
staring as you breathe the icy cold air.

To that lonely big lake,
you know you belong.
You were in there once—
we all were.

What's your lake story?
Would you care to think?

Of the Puppy, the Dog

There was a little puppy at the end of my street.
Sweet little thing.
I fed it once—just that once.
Brave little one when I met him first.
He feared no one.

For years, he saw me, and I, him.
We barely spoke, yet I knew him; he knew me.
He'd watch from 100 yards away,
a glance, then he'd look away.

He watched all—
the people, the pigeons, everything around.
He grew old,
but kept his borders.

Sweet and old, it became routine to share that glance.
Then, one evening, he was gone.

A day passed, then a week.
What stories they had when they spoke of him!

That brave heart—if he could speak,
what would he have told?
A chapter unread,
a book unwritten.

What stories would he have told?

Of the King with Rings

There lives an old tree—
over 5,000 years it's lived.
Gran Abuelo, they call it.
What whispers must it have heard?

When words weren't written,
what sounds would it have soaked?
Once sap, now sapient,
wonder the records it holds—

Cries and laughter,
nights of stars, and days of light,
bees and birds, and men and women—
what memories could it play?

Those rings it holds, like wrinkles on us,
they tested time—pressed in stories.
If those rings could speak, would you ponder
what stories would they tell?

Of the Saharan Sand

Long before time was spoken of,
there were specks of dust.
The world formed, then everything in it.
There was heat and pressure—things stuck,
and things broke.

Dust turned to rocks,
and broken rocks turned to grains of sand.
The oldest sands have seen millions of years.
They are truly the sands of time!

Nature's story—everything stores things.
The misery of things—nature's not a kind author.
Like words in a madman's journal,
nature played with sand—
with scorch, flood, wind, and dirt.

Wonder—of the first grains that broke,
if there's one still surviving?
If sands could talk—not to us—
could they have passed down stories?

If all the worlds were once but a few dense particles,
imagine all the stories a grain of sand could tell.
There are more stars than grains of sand, they say—
but then again,
who's heard what each has to say?

Of the First Drop

Of ancient tales of the absurd—
of elixir, of destruction,
oh, of everything said, there are stories of water.
It's been around a few billion years—
this frivolous compound—
a handful of stories speak of its origin.

Unspeakable amounts beneath our earth,
yet consider just what's on the surface.

Was the first drop scared?
Did it roll, unwilling to be pushed?
Is that why it trails wet?
Did it tremble as it froze?
Is that why it breaks?

Did it scream when it weathered?
Is that the sound when it's seared?
Of all the things you've done,
have you ever wanted to hear a spill?

If you do,
what stories do you imagine it would tell?

Of Destination

Ever been on a journey long?
You, a passenger, unaware of a stoppage.
A story so trivial,
most won't bat an eye!
Stay for a moment—
you, a passenger, restless with time!

You wait, and wait.
You ask your elder, *how long till we stop?*
Perhaps there's no need to relieve.
Perhaps it's just boredom.
Imagine no stories to linger—
passing through endless nothing.
You count your seconds—wonder, *how long!?*

You ask again, again, and again.
They say, right around.
Right around, more nothing.
Right around, just another bend.

You may have been through those roads—maybe not.
You count seconds nevertheless.
Were you ever that kid?
Are you that now?

Imagine the first ever particle thrown out—
the big bang that scattered, well, everything!
The first particle ever,

still rushing through space,
making time—
not making good time.
Making time—the frustrating journey through
everything!

All to just get to that halt,
to step down to a world of nothing,
stretch, relieve, just take in a breath of anything!
From the beginning—
that first trillionth of a second,
do you think that particle knows much at all?
Or is it just warp speed of nothing?

If you ever ask it,
would it tell the story?
The story of all that's ever been?
Or maybe just the story of itself—
the story of all it's ever been through?

Or is it too far-fetched?
Would imagination stretch that much?
Would there really be a story it could tell?
Would you have a story you'd want to tell?

Of the Infants

There's a legend that babies speak a language.
They hear, listen, and understand.
The legend is that they forget those words,
forget when they start learning what's taught.

Legends be mocked.
But humor, though,
should they be true—
what happy cackles would they be telling?
Or what scary scars would they want healing?

People are paintings on canvases.
You see a Rembrandt, you see the painting.
Do you ever see the lines drawn, rubbed away—
away in the background, dull but marked?

People are like canvases too.
The painting you see is portrayed,
rubbed, righted, and reeled.

Walk out and see—there are stories everywhere.
Like those paintings, so beautiful—
maybe not adorning the canvas—
maybe simply hanging heavy on it.

Believe that legend.
Would you know what the toddler says?
Slate just fresh, wiped just a bit.

Do you think they'd want to tell it?
If you ask, would they spill?
Would you ever care to hear?
Let them be mundane or full of rivets—
would you have the heart to bear?

Of the Quiet Bonds

You see them once here, once there.
It's no moonlit sky, nor pouring rain—
It's just two people.
You see them old, you see them young,
you see them sitting, arms brushing.

They're slow, maybe loud.
One's tall, maybe one's small.
Maybe they're just perfect.
They sound swell and smell of garden.

You see them, you hate them, you love them,
maybe ignore them—they're there.
There's struggle behind, there's care,
there's respect and pain.
There's perhaps spite, regret, or remorse—
but there's togetherness.

Maybe there's truth, there's commitment.
Maybe there's love.

Love—do you wonder what that's like?
Have you been there?
Are you in there now?
Does it really matter?
It's no rhetoric—it doesn't.

Do you know there are stories to tell?
My friend, of love or hate,
of compulsion for compassion—
drama, one would think.
Drama, it probably is.

Every soul you look down upon,
every pretty face you look up to—my friend,
there are stories to tell.

They say time and tide wait for none.
Life and love don't wait for themselves!
There'll come a time,
you'll be shown love.
Maybe you've already been there.
Even if it's not yours.

Would you care to relive it?
Would you care to tell it?

Of Time

When you're racing against time—
not to get ahead,
not to beat the clock—
you race against yourself—
run with only one thought:
one goal, one person.

Racing against yourself, my friend,
you know you're racing against nothing.
There are no cheers—
just you.

Through the painful pace,
admit, it's painful.
But this pain?
It'll fade away.

You race against yourself—
not to lose; but sometimes you will.

Fighting the battle, not the war,
you keep fighting.
If you are racing and they're not waiting,
are they worth your fight?
Are they worth the wait?

Would they ever tell your story?
Of your time, of your love?

Do you think they'll talk of your time?
Or would you be a story to throw aside?
My brother, sister, them—respect your story.

If I care to ask you now, of your story,
would you care to tell?

Of Echoes of the Sea

All you've heard are stories of struggle—
yet they all took the trouble to get through!
I'm a hill-grown man.
I'll die a hillfolk.
The one thing I'll die jealous of—
is not being born of the sea!

Have you ever sat on the shores?
Have your ears hurt?
Have you listened to what the waves say?
There's pain, love, life.
There's the world ahead.

Life on the ocean, life near one,
is perhaps the afterlife for the rest of us.
Life is not what we're erring now.
Do you know, though?

Have you heard the story from the seas?
Not of the seas—from the seas.
Life is on the ocean!
Life's that float!

Have you ever wondered what that's like?
Are you living that now?
Do you know what the story there's like?

Of Last Breath

Know what it's like to hold the last breath?
Have you been near one?

When you look at someone,
know that's the last you'll speak—
with them, maybe not of them.
Do you now know what life's like?

Think of those last breaths.
Do you hear them?
Do you hear what stories they tell?

Would you care to just hear?
You're not to talk.
Are you fit to just hear?

If you did, would you care to remember?
Stories—those stories to tell!

Of Your People

The rush and the run!
Around cacophony and chaos,
do you ever see—there are stories to tell?

That beggar,
the cop, that kid on the sidewalk!
What do you see?
Do you not hear their stories?

The proud lawman,
the feminist, the fighter in all,
the cart pusher, the shoe shiner,
the pretty girl with the scar,
the old man with wisdom in his eyes,
the dry smile of that trafficked girl,
the loud cry of that unheard baby,
the light you thought shined bright,
and your heart that I just broke in shards!

Forgive me—but do you see them?
Those stories though—I don't explore.
Those stories though—think now and think again!
Do you hear them?

Of Minutes

In six, what can you tell?
Of strength?
Of life at low?

Would you then talk of pain and struggle,
of worries and vanities, of those of might?

If six minutes is all you have,
what story would you tell?

Would you sum your stories?
Would you think it vain?
Would you tell it still?

Of Pain

Takes a moment to see,
yet more to feel.

Takes scores more to speak of it.
When it's not you who's fighting it,
and it's not you causing it—
it's harder to see.
But it hurts.

Faith hurts. It hurts.
It's hard to hear
when pain paints stories.
But it's there.

Would you ever care to see
what pain speaks of?
Those stories run thicker than blood—
and they hurt.

Like molten fire in your veins.
Like barbed wire for nerves.

If they ever tell you,
would you lend an ear?

Of Chimes and Whistles

Recall that last breeze?
Did it brush through your hair?

Winds move minds—they move might.
Stay, I'll tell you a story.

Winds don't see borders.
They're why wings work.
Demented yet wise, they speak truth.

Recall the day it went quiet?
Oh, how you yearned for that hum!
Winds play minds—they play might.
You still stay! Your patience, I adore!

Winds have heard it all—
from the first-ever story to this one,
of those undone and those condemned.

They read it all when they ruffle
and sing clues when they whistle.
What do they hush when they kiss the chimes?
Have you ever asked?

Of the Moon, On the Moon

There's an old story
of a woman weaving on the moon!

Moon in the sky,
for as long as we've known.

Have you ever thought, though,
of what dragged it to our door?
They speak of Theia,
they speak of a bump.
Was it inebriation?
An intoxicated planet rolling the wrong plane?

Or was she a lone soul,
seeking warm solace,
who ended up shattering herself?

Is that Theia on the moon,
weaving stories to live?
If there really is a woman with a loom,
is she the one threading space?

Maybe all old wives' tales were true.
Maybe—except for this one.
And if this is true too,
what stories does it tell?

Of Lion Man

Löwenmensch—the lion man—
the oldest statue in the world.

Ivory-made, 35 millennia ago,
who paid whom to sculpt?

Statues are cruel, aren't they?
Limbs without movement,
eyes can't shut, lips don't speak,
but ears—ears, maybe they hear!

Statues are cruel.
To see stories—to hear stories
yet to tell no one!
Perhaps the sculptors heard those screams,
but they built, regardless!

Statues are cruel.
They capture a moment,
but leave no voice.
They stand—silent, unmoving—
while stories fade,
fading into time.

If the Lion Man could speak,
would he maybe prefer to be a she?
If he's a she,
what stories would she tell?

Memories to Dwell

Mind the Memories

They say the mind is cluttered—
focus must be practiced,
attention must be built.

They say, "*Empty your mind.*"
If it were that simple,
Buddhas would bloom everywhere.

The mind, a pool of murky water—
even when still,
the depths stir with layered memories.

Memories that nourish thoughts.
Do you see?
Without them, are you even real?

Language, taste, feeling—all born of memory.
Memories maketh man, woman,
and every soul beyond pronouns.

So make amends while you can,
while the echoes of what was
still shape the you that is.

Scaping Mind

The mind is a landscape—
habits carve its contours.

Like rivers ebb and flow,
thoughts shape curves, leave craters.

The thoughts you dwell on form habits.
The memories you revisit forge paths.

The more you walk them,
the more you're bound to tread them.

Feed on joy, you turn radiant.
Linger on sorrow, misery deepens.

Memories shape your many selves,
for you hold multitudes within.

Even the most desolate hearts
remember a smile or two.
Build on those; make life worthwhile.

But pine for pain, anger, or fear—
they become too familiar, too inviting.

The mind, a creature of habit,
dwells where it knows to hurt.

Sometimes, it fuels your journey,
keeps you vigilant—on guard.

What you feed it
is what flourishes within.

You risk losing the feast of life
to the sweetness of vengeance or despair.

For the mind's true strength
lies in its taste for variety—
a palette that deserves richness.

Let not pain and fear dominate;
let hope, joy, trust, and strength flow.

Let the landscape be winding, rugged,
but full, balanced, whole.

Only then are you complete.

To be mindful is less an art—
it is a habit, practiced and tuned.

Shape it well, and in time,
you become someone's cherished memory.

Language of Memory

Do you remember learning a language?
The first words, the letters—
curves and lines that felt so foreign.
Do you recall how daunting it was?

The first time you wrote your name,
it felt like it belonged.
That's the secret of etching memories—
plug your everything into it.

Sounds and sights, once alien,
bloom into worlds unexplored.
Without knowing,
you've begun a journey.

But do you remember that moment?
Perhaps not—
not the first word, nor the first letter.
Yet the language remains.

It may be the only tongue you speak,
but it shaped you,
carving memories deep.
The more you seek, the more you see.

This is the beauty of language:
not just words with enchanting meanings,
but tools to build memories,
commands to redeem experiences.

Memories Committed

We all yearn to relive the firsts—
the first bike ride, the first recital,
the first crush, the first visit to the park,
the first swim, the first New Year's Eve.

Remembering them exaggerates the joy—so be it.
They truly bring back smiles in the dark.

But if you could go back, would they feel the same?
Would there be urges to change?
Do orchestrated firsts leave marks as deep?
Perhaps the sense of success lingers still.

What do you yearn to relive now?
Of the many firsts, hold onto the one with the widest grin,
or the quiet calm that stilled all noise—
maybe the spark of triumph, no matter the size.

In these feeble attempts to savor time long gone,
we seek solace.
Our greatest strength is often ourselves.
These longings for the old days—
they aren't weaknesses;
they reflect our commitment.

For even unwittingly committing to memory,
is what drives us forward.

Let memories be your strength—yearn for more.
And go forth to make many more.

Breath of Memory

Count back down.
From here, as far into the past as you can go.
Breathe, close your eyes—let your mind race.

Do you feel it?
The throb in your head,
air weaving through your nostrils, into your throat?

All that you've been through—
are you not proud?
Proud to simply be here, alive,
able to read these words?

What's that one memory lingering now?
Is there more? Good on you.
Let it rise—
pain, joy, yearning or desire.

Even the faintest memories—
distant, vague, maybe imagined—
they shaped you.
Even the ones you made up shaped you still.

Do you wish to be more?
Then go—
go make more memories.

Memories Inherited

There's an old bridge across the river—
broken, out of commission,
but still standing.

Every time I drive by,
walk around,
or simply think of it,
I think of my father and his brother.

As teens, they'd jump off it—
into the river,
a 60-meter drop.

Neither of them is here now.
I wasn't there with them then, clearly,
but I remember it,
as though I were.

Memories don't always have to be yours.
Sometimes, you live what you hear.
Sometimes,
those are the best memories you'll ever have.

Life to Instill

Life's Someone

I wouldn't kill.
Not for revenge, not for defense.
Not because it's the greatest sin,
not just because it's cruel.

But because I know this:
everybody is someone's someone.
Nobody is truly a nobody.
No matter how bad they are,
no matter how insignificant.

I know how much I need my people—
even the ones I haven't spoken to in years,
even those miles away.
I know how deeply I miss those I've lost—
even when we shared so little in life.

And you—
you must not take a life either.
Not for anger, not for pride.
Because when you take a life,
you take away someone's someone.

A brother, a sister,
a friend, a rival, a teacher.
You take them from a world
that still needs them—and it always will.

And even if you think they deserve it,
their absence will haunt
the lives they've touched.

Think of your own people—
the ones who ground you,
the ones you love,
the ones you've lost.

Would you want that taken from you?
Would you want someone to vanish,
leaving only echoes behind?

Life is fragile,
life is intertwined.
To kill is to sever a thread
that binds us all.

So don't.
Don't take that away from someone.

Life's Forward

When do you really know it's your time?
You pass through life like a fleeting cloud,
showering where you're needed—
and then you disappear.

But must you?
Must you always vanish?
Why not linger, just for a moment,
to see yourself as a constant?

You've learned, unlearned,
broken rules one day,
then the next,
again and again.

Is it others, or is it you?
The mirror demands strength—
to face yourself,
to ask: *Who am I, truly?*

You've done what you could,
maybe just enough,
yet the world spins onward,
unaffected, unchanged.

Where does this self-worth come from?
You've lived a few decades now,
yet the years blur, forgotten.

But remember this:
you are not the perfect being you imagined—
and that's okay.
Imperfection is not failure;
it is proof that you've lived.

Your pain is a guide,
a whisper from evolution,
saying: "*Grow forward, not back.*"
Not to repeat,
but to learn.

Honor those who've stood by you—
their kindness, their strength.
Be grateful,
for they've weathered your storms.

And when the time comes to evaporate,
let it be with grace.
Not as a surrender,
but as a gift of life well shared.

Fighting hurts, yes.
But fighting can also transcend—
not to erase the past,
but to shape the future.

Feel your breath now,
inhale the world as it is.
And remember—
don't wish it away.

Life in Now

At 16, I never thought I'd miss being 4.
At 20, I didn't miss being 15.
At 30, I missed being 20.
At 40, will I miss being 35?

The past sometimes seems greener.
But even if it was, it wouldn't be right to go back—
it wouldn't feel the same.
Life doesn't let you relive—
it only moves forward.

You look back and yearn,
but only because of today.
If not for today,
who you are means little.

Today, my friend, is where life happens.
Today is yours—
as tomorrow will be.

Today and tomorrow—
the only places where life breathes.
Yesterday?
It's a memory—a shadow of what was.
Don't let it hold you hostage.

Life is here,
in the breath you take now,
in the choices you make today.

Yesterday has done its part.
Today is your turn to shape what comes next.
Live it fully—
because life always moves forward.

Life's Abyss

So what ties you to them?
What pulls at your heart,
even when they're far, unseen, or unknown?

It's that quantum thread—
a resilient line across the abyss,
an invisible pull,
keeping you both in sync—
even across infinite distances.

If insanity is the abyss we choose to traverse,
let the speed of light guide the way.
If the journey feels unmoored,
let the void itself become your anchor.

Keep drifting—
through the vastness, through the void.
You'll always find your way.
Keep drifting—
until the thread pulls you closer.

Maybe, one day,
you'll find another drifter.
Your drifter.
The quantum thread pulling you near,
until you collide—
speed dizzying, potential buzzing,
a fusion of all that is unknown.

Perhaps that's how it all began—
a collision of drifters pulled by the thread,
the first spark of existence,
the abyss becoming light.

Because you never imagine
without first being inspired.

And if it all started by mistake,
is it wrong
to believe it still holds meaning?

Life's Paradox

You can't miss what you've never had.
You can't yearn for what you've never felt.
You can't wish for what you don't believe is possible.

Life, from nature's view, is existence—
a spark that endures.

For the heart,
life is love—
a connection that binds.

For love,
life is care—
holding, being held, and existing.

For existence itself,
life is grind—
a chase that never ends.

Life isn't a dream,
just as dreams aren't imaginary.
Dreams repocket memory;
nightmares are therapy—
unasked for, yet needed.

And when you think
you can miss what you've never had,
life is then untrue, it is imaginary.

Life isn’t absence; it’s presence.
It’s what you hold,
what you endure.

Life is all of this,
and none of it.
It’s the paradox you live.

Life's Love

Love is ambivalent—
It breaks you open,
yet turns you whole.

Heart-wrenching, heart-warming,
both at once, or one following the other.
It steals your breath,
yet teaches you to breathe.

A glance across a crowded room,
a smile that lingers for decades,
a quiet touch, a loud goodbye—
universes held together,
universes torn apart.

They say love is chemical—
a logical trick of the brain,
oxytocin, dopamine, serotonin—
molecules that bind hearts and minds.
Yet how can logic explain,
a yearning that spans lifetimes?

It's in the laughter shared over nothing.
In the silence that speaks volumes,
in the ache of waiting,
and the joy of finding.

Love defies itself.
It is raw, messy, perfect.
It transcends distance,
lives in the spaces between words,
and fills the voids words can never reach.

Love is the warmth of a hand held tight—
sometimes, an everlasting pain—
the breaking of a heart,
and the unbreakable promise
of life lived in its glow.

Life's Seed

A seed, in its quiet eagerness,
longs to sprout, to stretch and reach,
to become part of something larger.
In its smallness, it dreams of the sky,
of branches, leaves, and roots that intertwine.

It's the same beauty we see in children,
mimicking adults, their eyes wide with wonder.
Their overwhelming reactions—
that desire to grow, to take part in it all.
It's a reflection of the seed's yearning
to become what it was always meant to be.

But the seed doesn't do this alone—
it relies on the earth, the sun, the rain,
each one offering something vital,
a conversation only nature knows,
a language of light, soil, and water.

They speak to each other—
the seed to the soil,
soil to the sun,
water to the air.
Bees and birds, too, are part of this dance,
and we—
we've forgotten how to listen.

Did we ever know how to hear them?
Or have we always been too busy
to hear the soft murmurs of the world around us?
Perhaps we're not meant to hear them.
But we are meant to witness their journeys,
to marvel at the life they create.

For in their quiet speech,
in their reaching for the light,
they remind us—
we too are part of this dance.
We too are waiting to sprout,
to become what we were always meant to be.

Life's Lived

A life lived well isn't defined by rules,
nor by the hands that shaped it,
but by the dynamism it carries—
the ever-shifting dance between growth and stillness.

It's in the moments of reckless joy,
like the first drop that broke the stillness;
in the quiet, contemplative pauses,
as silent as the whispering winds that crossed the
lake.

It's not a straight line,
but a winding road full of unexpected turns,
like the path of a seed yearning to become a tree,
relying on the sun, the soil, and the unseen threads of
the earth.

Life is like the stories we tell—
it changes with each telling,
each experience layering the one before,
like rings in the old Gran Abuelo tree,
holding memories of lives we'll never fully know.

There's beauty in the struggle,
in the uphill battles that test our strength,
and in the ease of a day well spent,
like the quiet moments when time stood still
and the ocean whispered stories to those listening.

A life lived well is not about perfection.
It's the mistakes, the lessons, the growth,
the echoes of laughter shared with strangers,
the warmth you felt in the presence of love,
even if you never had the words for it.

It's about living fully,
even in the mundane—
like the forgotten roads where memories still wander,
in the spaces between breaths,
where the moments we almost missed
hold the most meaning.

A life lived well is not bound by the past,
nor obsessed with the future.
It is present—
here, in this moment,
where everything converges,
where the quiet speaks louder than words,
and the stories we've lived whisper to each other.

Live.